DECLARATION

by Jeff Roush

©2014 by Jeff Roush

Acknowledgments

This collection, my first, could not have happened without the support and inspiration of my family and friends. My wife, Lori, and my sons, Ben and Timmy, help me find ways to smile every day, even (and sometimes especially) when they are driving me completely nuts. My parents continue to blow my mind with the strength and love they show. My siblings have spent a lifetime pointing out the reasons I should be laughing at myself; for this I am grateful. And my friends inspire me every day, reminding me how fortunate and blessed I am to have them in my life.

Particular thanks go as well to those who have contributed editing and advice toward this collection: Marie Trevino, Fritz Swanson, and Dory Stewart. I appreciate your help, whether delivered gently or via a needed kick in the hindquarters.

Contents

Life 7
    Wide Eyes 8
    Sunday Destruction 9
    To My First "I Love You" 10
    Friday's Razor 11
    The Ducks of the Ottawa 12
    This Once Was Home 13
    Reading *Walden* 15
    A Deciduous Mind 18
Liberty 19
    The Hiding Place 20
    Messiah in Waiting 21
    Afternoon Escape 23
    Ruminations on Highway Feet 24
    Leading into Temptation 26
    Stolen Guilty Moments 27
    Gone Swimming 28
    The Weekend Before 29
Pursuit 31

American Dreamers 32
Don Quixote de la Suburb 34
Writing the Perfect Poem 36
Unspoken 38
GPS Relativity 39
To Eat a Peach 41
Chasing Music 42
Symphonic Suite for a Traffic Jam 44

Life

Wide Eyes

Your entire face is eyes,
big blue whirlpools
that pull in every
unnamed shape and
ever-new color,
your whole existence in
each moment,
each unblemished
discovery.
I watch and label
every moment:
"First Smile."
"Tummy Time."
"Giggled and Cooed."
"Rolled Over."
"Bumped into Dog and
Gurgle-Growled."
I peer from a lifetime
away, follow your
every mystery through
clouds of nomenclature.

Sunday Destruction

Early morning, late October.
A boy, six, watches,
nose poked through porch rails.

Mower and Daddy emerge,
roll irrevocably to tree,
pause at leaf-circle's edge—

then proceed with a guttural roar,
drown the boy's shouts as they
rip through brown, red, orange, yellow,

leave almost-monotonous mulched
green, seasoned by sun-sparked
flecks of colors that were.

To My First "I Love You"

I said "I love you"
and I meant it:
lost in light blonde locks,
big innocent eyes,
smiles that shattered
fragile panes of cynicism.
For months I pressed,
loosed my heart from my chest,
threw it at you because
I wanted you to have it,
thought you should want it.

I said "I hate you"
and I meant it:
I blamed you,
yelled in my head
and hit the road
one angry step at a time.
A five hundred mile summer
beat it out of me,
pushed it out with my sweat,
ground it under rubber outsoles
till I forgot to keep hurting
one hot midsummer morning
and I said "I'm over you."

Friday's Razor

Friday means a
new razor.
It gleams under
bathroom lights,
sharp and shiny.
Four blades
glide over
rough whiskers and
bare scar patches;
stubble disappears
under a magic swath.
Its path
catches at the
chin, tugs hairs,
nicks skin.
I finish with
smooth jaw and
jagged strips of metal
to make last
till next Friday.

The Ducks of the Ottawa

The river's sole unfrozen circle
lies still—
a cold Jacuzzi
for the ducks who never leave.
They land and ripple the pool,
swim its tiny circumference.
Fowl family members
squabble, bicker,
shake tail feathers,
chide the patriarchal drake
who blew the travel fund
again this year.

This Once Was Home

The drive in drops suddenly:
45, then 35,
just where I remember,
early obstacle from
radar-dodging teen years
when driving was part game,
part adventure, one piece of
in-the-moment idiocy
that brought speeding tickets,
summer romances,
a Master's degree.
To my left, a new former strip mall,
paint flaking off the shell,
where corn used to grow.
To the right, a pizza place
sits where it should, but
a different sign fronts it:
a new someone's old dream,
nestled between the pharmacy
that belongs three blocks
farther up the road and
the one-time Laundromat
that still boasts twenty
abandoned machines.
Turn from main drag to
neighborhoods, and
houses loom with

vague familiarity;
yards frame the right
shapes and strange,
homogenous siding,
wrap everything in
presque vu.
Across the street,
the neighbors' perfect lawn
grows wild, a *Jumanji* jungle
reaches out, grabs the
street with green tendrils,
threatens to invade
the house that was home.

Reading *Walden*

His first read:
all angst and gangle,
words pushing through bangs
like sunlight between blind slats.
He stares at the book,
blue eyes unfocused, jaw set,
teeth gleaming silver.
Hair swishes as he shakes his head
at a weird Harvard guy
living in the woods
eating woodchucks.

Two years later, tweed-clad professors
force the next read,
pour ideas into wide-eyed heads
that nod with erudition:
kids who now know
they know nothing.
"I too want to live deliberately,"
he says from beanbag chair recesses,
tossing late-night insouciance out amid
empty pizza boxes and
scattered popcorn kernels.
"Sheltered no more."
"Free and uncommitted.
"Life of solitude."

Grad school brings
wispy chin hairs
pulled to a fauxtee;
he tugs while he reads.
By day he builds his
castles in the air,
dances without music,
tells everyone he follows
a different drummer,
will live as no one has before.
He tosses at night, sits up with
wild, tousled hair,
tells himself grass
still covers his path.

Ten years later grey locks
thin by the moment.
He turns through
dusty leaves,
respite from his life,
his quiet desperation.
The marginalia leap out
in black and blue ink,
semi-legible scrawls:
"Transcendentalism";
"Religious or Spiritual?";
"Yawp as defiance";
"I can't believe
I'm reading this shit again!";

"Compare Self-Reliance";
"Me too..."
Eyes dance back and forth,
edges to text and back;
a twitch teases a smile
on a wiser savage
treading water in his
bottomless pond.

A Deciduous Mind

Spring's first buds
bloom in green,
grow full and thick,
at once dense and
delicate.
Soon green
bursts in red,
surges in orange,
emerge in yellow.
The burgeoning collage
dazzles with depth,
obscures slow
baring of branches
till the inexorable
fade to brown,
drift to grey,
float to white.

Liberty

The Hiding Place

On the playground a concrete tube
sufficed—simple, solid,
both ends open:
lookout, escape route.
Three lay together, perpendicular;
Shifting winds just meant
a move to the next tube,
a brief scramble to evade
January blasts.
Footsteps boomed through,
small feet pounded like
bass drumbeats:
chase and flee,
happy shouts and gasps,
giggles trilling above.
I kept a close watch,
peeked around the edges,
listened for discovery's hush or
drumroll footsteps,
all the while wrapped in
cold, concrete comfort.
I never doubted my senses or speed,
my easy escape from closing footsteps
or bitter, shifting winds.

Messiah in Waiting

Twelve years old, Jesus spoke up—
then went silent for eighteen years,
doing God knows what:

a timeline of miracle highlights
and ascendant deadlines,
a melody for millions that

ignores the tacit interlude.
Almost two decades hammering,
black-and-blue thumbs throbbing

through clumsy adolescence,
gangly arms and legs
looking for their rhythm?

Or honing catch phrases,
"cat-burglars of men"
just missing with Mark.

He'd hide in His room,
the ultimate Misunderstood Teen,
but with all the fish He could eat.

Whither the parents' plight?
"But I'm the Son of God!"
"You still have to wash the dishes,

clean your room, and—
don't give me that look!
I'll beat your Holy Behind!"

The Gospels skip the
Party Years, when He jammed to
pipes, lyres, and trumpets,

cracked up apostles-to-be
every time He insisted
His mom was a virgin,

mystified teen Matthew and Luke
because no one ever saw Him
smuggle in the wine—

Boone's Farm quality in those days.
But the Savior honed his powers,
built toward the Big Day

He stepped from the shadows,
the Official Story picking up again
when He finally got the drinks right.

Afternoon Escape

A simple hand-switch,
too casual—

golden retriever bursts loose.
Hair ruffles in the wind,

jowls flap,
ears flop,

front and back paws
cross in bound after bound,

tongue dangles at
laughing snout's left.

His face turns, taunts.
The leash trails in the air,

deceptively close, and I stumble
after, laughter and obscenities

blend to cacophony.
My right arm stretches,

Fingers wriggle—
but never grasp.

Ruminations on Highway Feet

They titillated at first:
bare skin and colored nails
teasing horny teen me,
toes curling, beckoning
from dashboards and open windows.

Like the apocryphal fruitcake,
I once thought them
a single foot,
hopping from car to car,
seeing the sights.

But some proved smooth, some hairy,
some short, some long,
and one with two short toes,
cowering half-digits
dwarfed by three tall brethren.

Do they run from shoes,
dank, sweaty, dark?
Trapped all day,
seize a moment,
leap to freedom?

Or maybe to open air,
to the sun's caress,
to wind's whoosh through,

the body's ugly stepchildren
rising, flexing, unfurled?

Both, more likely:
the past always chases,
musty memories in sweaty pursuit
while freedom pulls toward
air and another tomorrow.

Leading into Temptation

I stride along a
cement walk and
glance over at
plush grass,
streaked with leaves of
orange and gold.
I jump at the
crackle under
wing-tip, and
my imagination—
seizing opportunity in
distraction—
darts into the field,
throws shoes and
suit behind,
laughs as he
tramples and rolls
and crunches the ground.
I watch him
play; my mouth
curls briefly upward
before I trudge ahead.

Stolen Guilty Moments

Urgency raps at
every moment's door:
calendars and deadlines,
mealtimes and playdates.
Every delay looms,
grips the heart
through the throat,
clenches, squeezes,
forces my hand to the phone,
directs constant calibration.
But tonight, I linger:
I pull the car in;
ignore exhaust that
curls up, dissolves into
neighborhood air;
glance at window lights
that accentuate
evening's steady creep;
reach for the radio and
turn it up,
nudge back at a world
that pushes inexorably on.
For a stolen fifty-seven
seconds I lean back,
loosen my tie,
close my eyes,
float.

Gone Swimming

My body drinks;
I wait.
Finally—
wobble, slump,
jerk, and fall—
cheek hits bar counter
with a squishy smack.
I ooze out the left ear,
grey and pink sliding
over purple face,
and leap,
splash into the
unconsumed half of
martini number three.
Gin and vermouth droplets
fly in all directions;
jiggle on the counter;
slide down yawning
glass-edge; and
drip slowly over
gently snoring
Rudolphian nose.

The Weekend Before

Saturday night:
dirt and grass lie underfoot,
wind pushing evening's chill
through my jacket.

Tonight stars shine,
their only obstruction
a hazy penumbra
softening the almost-full
moon's edges.

Tonight crickets chirp,
a song profanity punctuates
when tent poles slip
and canvas collapses
again.

Tonight the creek laughs,
splashes over rock and branch,
sloshes ten feet away
from campfire crackle and glow.

Tonight shadows reign,
stretch across the world;
a million sounds and shapes
blanket Monday morning's specter:

a hospital waits,
stark and white, stinking of
disease and Purel.
Pricked veins and scalpels,
old magazines and dashing doctors
loom, inevitabilities
pushed off the edges of tonight.

Pursuit

American Dreamers

"You can have anything you want
if you follow your dreams."
The words settled in,
repetition mimicked truth—
but dreams in our house
led elsewhere.

Many nights I dreamed
my knit panda with the big nose
rose up to chase me,
a recurring nightmare I never connected
to stifled giggles
from the bunk below.

At five, post-Dracula movie,
I dreamed of inching down the hallway,
back pressed to the wall
because I knew Dad's guitar case
would creak open, smoke would hiss out,
and the vampire would attack.

My big sister once confessed
through a mouthful of metal
she dreamed she was Leader One:
the sleek grey jet,
leader of the Go-Bots,
poor man's Optimus Prime.

My little sister dreamed
I stole her blankie,
accusation sputtered out
under red and puffy eyes.
Yeah, I did it.
Two was old enough to let go.

And last night, again, a free-fall:
wind blasted past my ears;
clothes whipped up against me
while greyscale shapes streaked past;
I mouthed a voiceless shout;
and I woke.

Don Quixote de la Suburb

Morning begins with alarm bleat
too early, three times over,
then a coffee-ward lurch.

Kids bounce in, demand
breakfast and games and
Functional Daddy.

Deadlines loom;
calendar and email scream,
reach through phone screen,

tug my pajama collar
toward work tasks
carved into six-minute intervals,

their betweens stuffed with
meals and check-ins,
blood tests and insulin—

a dozen tiny pricks,
annoyances to accumulate
for the rest of my life.

Laundry beckons,
piles rise even when they fall,
spill over their own edges

with unmatched socks
like the baking soda volcano
I finished at three a.m.

A frenetic shower,
a haphazard shave, and
a backwards t-shirt:

I am ready, ready to launch,
pushing forward,
working and stumbling toward
a Someday that will not come today.

Writing the Perfect Poem

This will really be the one.
A moment in words,
captured perfectly—
no, scrap the adverb.
Captured. Yes, that's it:
simplicity itself,
a lexicological sunset,
red verbs layered through
orange nouns,
splashed across the
canvass page,
hints of purple adjectives,
moving across on
chemical-infused clouds,
a coffee imagination
if you will.
No, not if: you WILL.
Wait, that doesn't even
make sense.
Stop at imagination;
let the coffee
speak for itself.
Now, action:
the reader, a plane, streaks across,
white streaming behind it.
He slashes—
no, she slashes

(no masculine prejudice
in the Perfect Poem),
bifurcates poem from intent.
Art imitates life, you know.
But wait:
A speck of skydiver emerges:
the poet-pilot has
ridden the asymptote too long,
leaps out, defies the line, and
disappears, immersed in
ethereal perfection.

Unspoken

"I love the smell of
fresh asphalt in the morning,"
I almost tell the approaching beauty,
amid jackhammer rattles and
thick, tarry fumes that
hang in the air
like the doubts choking my nerves.
"You're beautiful" stops before it can start,
smashed against a bulldozer.
"Do you have the time?"
leaps from my larynx,
falls into a pothole,
sends green ripples across
oil pooled inside.
Phrases fly silently until
my charming smile fades,
flatlines while she passes
obliviously by.

GPS Relativity

I will arrive at 3:37 this afternoon,
in four hours and eleven minutes—
unless I streak past speed limits,

slam the accelerator to beat my
time, or just because
I don't like the look of the

bald punk in the black Camaro and
need to dust him;
unless Starbucks beckons,

pulls me from the highway,
caffeine begging to
pile on top of adrenaline;

unless construction barrels
sprout in front of me,
lined for miles while

one worker leans to support
his bulldozer and seven burly colleagues
drink coffee and stare at concrete;

unless I give in and stop
to sate hunger's deep,
cavernous rumble, or to piss.

With each stop and each surge
time wobbles, 3:37 morphs
to 3:29, 3:41, 3:38,

till I set my jaw, ignore
cramps and boredom, and finish
my last hour in fifty-two minutes.

To Eat a Peach

Do I dare? A peach—
ripe, plump, mine—
I cannot resist.

The fuzz touches first,
a soft, unfamiliar
tickle under my nose,

brushes, teases
before teeth and lips
sink into tender flesh.

Juice sweet and
thick rolls over
tongue, lips, fingers, chin.

I consume to the core,
devour and savor,
take—and crave more.

Chasing Music

A saxophonist dashes
through the parking garage,
charity gala far behind.
He tugs his bowtie,
opens two buttons,
stalks past immaculate
Mercedes and BMWs that
gleam under security lights.
The last staid Dorian tones
linger like rancid milk,
dousing his mind as
he flings open the
rusty van door,
dumps shiny performance sax
and grabs Betsy:
dinged, drab, perfect.
He jumps in,
clutching her as the engine roars.
Balding tires squeal as he escapes—
to the old town,
to holes in the wall,
to scents of stale beer
and sweat and sadness,
to ears for real jazz,
to honks and growls,
to dissonance and discord,
to frenetic tension and

the raw, raunchy release
choked back through a
night of sycophantic,
antiseptic polish.

Symphonic Suite for a Traffic Jam

I. Allegro non troppo

Rain begins on asphalt—then to
snare drum roll: hood, windshield, roof.
Car accelerando pushes
over entrance ramp to highway.
Home awaits; dinner's cooking
forty highway miles away.
Weave through five o'clock rubato,
left, then right, then left again,
always moving forward, homeward:
skirting exit ramp delays,
older drivers, local yokels.
NPR blasts Shostakovich—
till radio traffic interjects:
bridge is flooded; all lanes stopped.
Look for exit—too late.
Tail lights loom ahead, blinking
quickly first, then lingering, stretching,
holding—ritardando in red,
rolling to thousand-car fermata.

II. Lento

Chaotic stillness:
inch by half-hour
cars ooze forward
between caesuras.

The interstate
parking lot waits,
windows opening,
word trickling back:

"Highway flooded."
"Highway closed."
"Five cars stuck."
"Poor stupid bastards."

So I wait,
forty miles and
undetermined
hours between
here and home.

III. Scherzo

BEEP BE-BE-BEEP! HONK HONK HONK!
Trapped in a line-up with
deadlines to meet, just an
impotent idiot
one of a thousand in
traffic morass on a
highway undone.
Beep be-be-beep! Honk honk honk!
Creep to the right to the
left to the right again,
look for an opening,

gap between cars when some
driver forgets to go,
only to stop again—
stuck to the spot while the
clock ticks on, rolling past
time to meet, time to eat,
time to play, time to sleep.
BEEP BE-BE-BEEP! HONK HONK HONK!
Deep in the night while I
sit.

IV. Vivace

Ahead, the movement starts:
ignitions turn; the lead
cars launch out, vault ahead.
The followers trail behind,
slow stretch along the road
like surging revolution,
inevitable release
that tension forces out.
My car at last breaks free—
lurches forward at ten,
twenty, forty, sixty,
shackles strewn behind with
the flood-stalled and the fender-bent,
lingering casualties I
blaze past at ninety-five,
delirious accelerando

pushing faster—
till downward glance restrains
again. I set the cruise
to safer speed, turn up
my music, settle in,
emerging stars above,
my coda the open
road ahead.

Made in the USA
Charleston, SC
06 May 2014